Single Parents
in Focus

Tom Beardshaw
Guy Hordern
Christine Tufnell

care
FOR THE
family
BUILDING FOR
TOMORROW

Care for the Family
PO Box 488
Cardiff
CF15 7YY

Dedication

To Andrew and all those like him -
who would love to help but aren't sure how.

"*This book should be put into the hands of everyone in church leadership. If even a few of its recommendations were put into practice, the lives of many single parents and their children would change dramatically.*"

Jill Worth

Author of Journey Through Single Parenting and editor of Home and Family, the magazine of the Mothers' Union

"*Single parents hate the phrase 'broken home'. Many of them work harder than conventional parents in creating a positive and balanced environment to nurture their children. In Britain more than one and a half million single parents look after over two and a half million children. They need the support of the whole community, not least because nearly half of them and their children live in poverty. A Church which takes seriously the biblical mandate to care for the fatherless must not ignore this reality. There is much to be learned from single parents and much to be gained from this thought-provoking and well researched book. I commend it to every church who wants to engage seriously with its local community.*"

The Right Rev James Jones, Bishop of Liverpool

Contents

Introduction

Annie left her husband after years of mental and physical abuse; she now looks after their two children in their two-bedroom terraced house.

Jo was a teenager who didn't realise that a night out clubbing would result in the daughter she now raises alone.

Since his wife divorced him and took the kids three years ago, Jim sees his children once a fortnight, at the weekend.

Bob has to shoulder much of the work of raising three children since his wife became an invalid after the birth of their twins.

Since her daughter died eight years ago, Sue has been raising her grandson alone.

In the United Kingdom, 1,760,000 single parents from all walks of life care for nearly 3 million children - about a fifth of all children.[1] Single parent families make up 7.65% of the total U.K. population - about 4½ million people. Churches are asking how they can effectively reach the mums, dads and children found within these single-parent homes.

Each one of us has, no doubt, known someone who is a single parent; perhaps you are one yourself. Perhaps you have regretted the difficulties that arise when the ideal combination of two parents for children is not in place. Maybe you have been struck by the talents and abilities of many single parents and wished they had more time to participate in the life of the church.

This book will help you to gain a greater understanding of the issue and develop a way forward in your concern and care for single parents. In it, we:

- Describe how people become single parents

- Ask "Why should the church care?"

- Open a window on to the world of a single parent, and ask what issues they face as individuals, parents and church-goers

- Offer some practical suggestions to churches to help them become more 'single parent family friendly'

- Give some practical ideas for individuals in churches who know single parents

- Ask you some questions to help you understand more clearly the situation of single parents in your area

- Provide details of organisations and resources that will help

It is our hope that reading this book will help you and your church fellowship to open your arms and hearts to single parents in your congregation and your area, and that this will help them reach their potential as individuals and parents.

1

Who is a Single Parent?

Every single parent family has its own story that has resulted in an individual parenting on their own. If you wish to care for the needs of a single parent, it is vital to know their story, as the issues they face and the needs they feel will be uniquely shaped by the course their life has taken.

What are the ages and number of children in the home?

This is obviously an important factor in determining the shape of the family's situation, and the issues that the adult faces as a parent. The youngest child in 62% of single-father-headed homes is 10 years or older. Single mothers often raise much younger children. The number of children in the family will obviously be a factor in determining the pressure on the parent, and sometimes, the amount of help available to them, as older children may join in helping to run the household.

What's their financial status?

One of the most common struggles for single parent families is the shortage of money. Of the 2.9 million children

living in one-parent homes in the U.K. in 1996, 41% of single
mums had an income of less than £100 per week.[2]

How supportive are their wider family and friends?

A supportive family network living close by can make an
enormous difference to a single parent as they go through
the trials of family life. Parents, other relatives or close
friends can provide much needed rest and opportunities for
adult contact by providing child care. The levels and kinds
of support that a single parent might appreciate from a
church will be largely shaped by the amount of support
they receive from their family and friends.

How did they become a single parent?

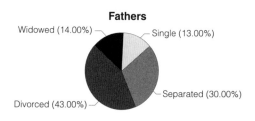

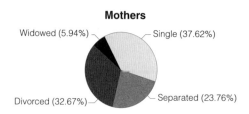

Source: Office for National Statistics Social Trends 1998

Divorce and separation of parents
In the last 30 years, the U.K. has seen an explosion in the number of marriages which end in divorce. In 1965, there were 40,000 divorces; in 1995 there were 170,000.[3]

A separated or divorced single parent will most probably have significant emotional hurts. Many struggle with feelings of inadequacy and failure, which can make new relationships much harder to form. Some single parents will have become Christians since their separation or divorce; for others, it has happened while they are Christians. Others in the local church may seem judgmental about the divorce and feel that in some way they do not deserve support. This can serve to reinforce the rejection that divorced single parents sometimes feel in the church.

For many families, divorce can be more traumatic than the death of a parent - there is no 'closure' to the situation, and tensions can often rumble on for years. There is also a sense of rejection, which does not occur when a parent has died. Children find the separation or divorce of their parents an especially difficult time. They are often bewildered and hurt, and many feel that somehow the situation is their fault. This can provide pastoral challenges for children or youth workers who know them.

When one of the parents - usually the father - is no longer able to live with their children, it is disturbing not only for that parent and the children, but also for the grandparents, who may have little or no access to their grandchildren. Sometimes the contact between the other parent and their children is regular, and sometimes erratic. While this book will focus on the experience of parents who are looking after their children alone, we must not forget those who are not able to live with their children.

Single, never married

The fastest growing group in the whole of U.K. society is single, never married, mothers. Many young women find themselves pregnant without the support or presence of the child's father. Young mums often live in poverty and lack opportunities to progress educationally or with their careers and vocations. Many people in churches are concerned that there are so many young women in this situation in society. Sometimes never married mums can feel that the church sees them only in this light - as a problem. As a result, they can face discrimination, misunderstanding and a lack of forgiveness from the church.

Death of a spouse

When a parent dies, not only does the family have to cope with enormous grief, but the remaining parent is left to raise the family alone and cope with the grief of the children. It is a daunting task, but if the family has been part of a church fellowship, there is usually a significant amount of support available to them, especially during this time of crisis. Often though, the support tails off when the immediate crisis is over, but this is the time when the family will start to face many of the same practical problems as other single parents. Sometimes, when a parent dies, a grandparent has to take over as parent - perhaps on their own. In all practical senses, they are living as single parents as well.

However someone might have ended up parenting on their own, crises and difficulty are likely to have been a part of their life's experience. Whether it is being deserted, the break-up of a marriage, or the death of a loved one, there are common struggles. Single parents have little spare time; they spend most of their time looking after children and often juggling their work and domestic tasks. This can leave them with very little energy, and there is no other adult around who can make them feel loved and valued. Very often, single parents face financial difficulties. Most single parents rely on social security and many have to cope in poor housing. Living in a society as affluent as ours, this can intensify the feelings of being an outsider. These factors can conspire together to create serious problems of isolation for someone who is on their own looking after children.

Single parents sometimes also express parenting problems that they attribute to being alone, when actually, many are general parenting problems that are faced by all parents. Often their isolation means that they are unable to share the issues they face with others, and they can think that they are alone in their problems. It is our firm belief at Care for the Family that one of the greatest threats to family life is the problem of isolation - the feeling of "I'm facing this problem alone" - which can turn an average family difficulty into a crisis. We hope that the understanding you gain from reading this book will help you and others in your church to take the first steps towards ending the isolation felt by many of the single parents that you know.

2

Why Should the Church Care?

Before we start looking at the lives of single parents and the issues raised, it is reasonable to ask, "Why should I spend time paying attention to this issue? What does the Bible say about our responsibilities as the body of Christ? How should we understand the issue of single parenting?"

What does the Bible say?

Single parents have always existed. In biblical times and throughout history, this was mainly the result of death and desertion. But single parents in earlier times had something that many do not have today: help from extended family. Many of today's single parents are left to accomplish their overwhelming tasks by themselves. That is why the help of the church has become so important. The phrase "single parent" is not specifically mentioned in Scripture, but widows and orphans are. Both Old Testament law and New Testament pastoral letters call for the people of God to look after those who have fallen on hard times. Scripture refers to our need to care for the widow more than 50 times, including:

> *"Do not take advantage of a widow or an orphan. If you do and they cry out to me, I will certainly hear their cry."* (Exodus 22:22-24).

> *"He [God] defends the cause of the fatherless and the widow, and loves the alien, giving him food and clothing." (Deuteronomy 10:18).*

> *"Learn to do right! Seek justice, encourage the oppressed. Defend the cause of the fatherless, plead the case of the widow." (Isaiah 1:17)*

> *"Religion that God our Father accepts as pure and faultless is this: to look after orphans and widows in their distress." (James 1:27).*

Meeting needs in a welfare state

One of the major differences between biblical times and contemporary Britain is the emergence of the Welfare State as the 'safety net provider', in contrast to the provision of family, community and church in biblical times. It's easy to think that because many single parents are given financial help by the state that their needs are being fulfilled. But single parents, in all their diversity, face a huge range of complex needs that cannot be met simply by money and housing, but by contact with people who are sensitive to the issues in their lives and are able to provide practical help.

Relationship breakdown

Churches are justified in their concern about the status of marriage in Britain today. Family breakdown has been an increasingly prominent feature of the social landscape in Britain. The high number of people who become single parents through divorce and separation is evidence of this. Churches have a responsibility to uphold marriage (Hebrews 13:4: "marriage should be honoured by all").

Some Christians find it confusing to relate to single parents, especially if their situation is the result of extra-marital sex or divorce. While seeking to be loving and accepting, people may also feel that there is something in the life of the single parent that they should disapprove of.

It is important to remember that as Christians, our communion with each other is possible because of the mercy and acceptance that God has shown to us. Mercy and grace from God mean that no one has to prove themselves before they can be acceptable.

It is especially important that those as vulnerable and sensitive to rejection as single parents should be shown the same mercy and acceptance by others in the body of Christ. This does not mean that churches should condone what they believe to be wrong, but simply that all of us, including single parents, need help and fellowship. Christians have a command from Jesus, to love, as he has loved us. That is, while we were still sinners, he died for us.

Growing in community

When a single parent comes into contact with a church fellowship, there is a huge potential for them to find a place of healing, where they can cultivate relationships that nurture and sustain their family. There are opportunities to find friends who will travel with them through loss and pain and help them to grow into a place where they are able to support others, perhaps those facing similar loss. Much of this depends on the reaction of those in the church fellowship to the single parents. All too often, human emotion can take over. Married people can feel threatened by single parents; pastors can feel ill equipped to deal with their needs, and the single parents themselves often stay hidden in the background. All too often, their situation is never thought about or spoken of, and nothing is done. If it is, it can often be on a very superficial level, with an unrealistic expectation that the problems will disappear overnight.

Churches can be amazing places in which people are comforted and helped in their relationship with the God of healing and restoration. God redeems the mistakes and hurts in all our lives, including those who are parents on their own.

Redeeming family life

It is well established in research literature[4] that the children of parents whose marriages have ended in divorce are more vulnerable to relationship breakdown of their own. There are many reasons for this, one of which is that they may have seen their parents use separation as the solution to conflict. One of the biggest predictors of divorce in a relationship is the poor handling of conflict.[5] Children need to be exposed to adults who are able to handle conflict positively, in a way that leads to reconciliation, forgiveness and growth, rather than escalating conflict and separation.

Children learn how to nurture healthy relationships when they grow up with an experience of family life that includes committed, loving relationships between adults, especially marriages. They can then grow up with the emotional security that gives them a firm foundation on which to build their own families. Without this, it is not impossible, but it is much harder. Learning how to deal with conflict can be especially difficult without a healthy role model. If their only model for dealing with conflict has been that separation is the solution, it makes it that much harder for children to grasp the idea that arguments can be resolved.

If a local church fellowship is a loving family of people united by one Father, they can provide the kind of extended family that will counteract this. One of the ways in which churches can help is to transmit a positive vision of married life to the children of single parents, by cultivating relationships between single parents and others in the congregation.

Living faith

The church is called to take care of people, and with compassion and love demonstrate the nature of true Christianity. In the church community, single parents ought to be able to find loving acceptance and healing for their hurts. One of the most important aspects of Christian involvement in society is undoubtedly at the local level, in churches such as your own, and it is within your local community that you really can make a difference. When God's people are active in the community, living as 'salt and light', they are a sign of his kingdom, his love and his justice. We can participate in his action in the world by siding with him to help those in distress, and demonstrating committed love that stands by people in their troubles. This is a vital expression of our faith. James makes this clear as he tells us that "faith by itself, if not accompanied by action, is dead" (James 2:17).

Even when we want to help, it can be difficult for those not in the situation to really understand the life of someone raising children on their own. To really understand takes thoughtfulness and imagination. To help in this process, we want to open a window onto the world of the single parent. In the light of this understanding, it may become easier to understand what God's justice and protection might mean to them in their daily lives.

3

Personal Issues

Biologically speaking, there is no such thing as a single parent, but in a single parent family, the biological parents are not united in the practical tasks of day to day parenting. Children know that they have both a father and a mother. When the mother and father are not together, the child has to learn a new way of relating to their parents.

Although a small minority of single parents choose to become parents without a partner, most are conscious of loss in their own lives. They also share in the loss in the lives of their children. The list of these losses can be overwhelming and it must be remembered that, in spite of the difficulties, not all single parents are overcome by their circumstances. It is, however, much harder for them as individuals and parents.

Loss of a parent and partner

For the single parent, this means loss of:

Companionship and shared decision making
Just as procreation is a joint enterprise, so is parenting. The joys and sorrows are designed to be shared and the pleasure and achievement lie partly in the shared experience of both

parents in the life of their child. Parenting and family life involves a continual process of decision making, from the routine planning of what to eat to the major decisions of school and career. Single parents have to make many decisions on their own without the balancing and complementary input from the absent parent.

Charlotte's losses:

- Husband - he left to be with another woman.
- Provider/money - he was the sole breadwinner.
- Home - the house came with the job.
- In-laws - they sided with their son.
- Self-esteem - he didn't want her, so how could others?
- Status - neither married nor single; "Where do I belong?"
- Expectations and dreams - to stay married for life, stability.
- Control - courts decided about their money.

Human love, including sexual love
Single parents are in the position of wanting to give out love to their children - whose need for love is not lessened by only having one parent - but not receiving intimate love themselves. This is one of the reasons why weariness can set in either periodically, temporarily or permanently.

Expectations, hope and trust

Most single parents have started out by trying to create a family. When relationships break down, those involved can sometimes emerge with a deep sense of failure and often a sense of having been betrayed. This inevitably affects other relationships. Their sense of failure can also often be accompanied by low self-esteem.

Friends and in-laws

One of the results of marital breakdown may be the loss of contact with in-laws who are of course also the children's grandparents. Just when the extended family is most needed, it will be most under threat. The same may be true of friends, who are prone to take sides in a marriage break-up, further weakening the support structure.

> One single parent summed up how many feel when she said that others see them as, "Second-class, scroungers, brought it on themselves, irresponsible, unfulfilled, sad, immoral - in short, a problem."

Status

Loss of status can be more acutely felt in the church than elsewhere. This can drive single parents into an exclusive group of their own, which reinforces their sense of loss, exclusion and low status.

Loss of resources

Home

If a relationship or marriage ends, it can also mean the end of the family home, which may have to be sold. Single parents often have to set up home again, with little income. Some find themselves in poor housing in areas with little communication, while others have to return to their parent(s), which may place additional strains on their family life.

Financial loss

Many single parents struggle to make ends meet financially. Two homes may have to be maintained when adults separate and most single parents rely on benefit. Balancing the need to provide for their family and spend time with their children can mean that a single parent is simply stretched in too many directions at once. Going out to work involves a loss of parenting, while staying at home to look after the children means living on benefits on the poverty line. Not everyone is blessed with budgeting skills and some may appreciate help.

Control

For many, there is also the feeling of being trapped in a situation they didn't choose and can't change. Those suffering a bereavement or divorce can feel their life is out of control. For many single parents, there will be the intervention of courts, and sometimes welfare officers and social workers. All of these may make major decisions affecting the parent's and children's lives for years. Sometimes these decisions will be against the parent's wishes.

Coping with loss

In all the areas of loss faced by single parents, there is much pain involved. Time is needed to mourn and readjust, but the demands of the children can override, so that the grief process remains incomplete. It is important for people facing such loss to be able to spend some time with other adults so that these feelings can be expressed safely.

There may be many difficult questions: "Why doesn't he love me any more?", "Why has he gone off with another woman?", "How can God be loving if he let my wife die?"

Depression and despair can come easily, as the past is painful, and the future can often look bleak. Often the identity and self-esteem of the parent is in danger of being lost. When so much of the life that they have built has collapsed, and the children need attention, there is little time to pay attention to becoming the person that God intends.

Emotionally and physically, all these pressures are very tiring, especially in the early years after a break-up or the death of a partner. The attitudes of many in society towards single parents also help to break their self-esteem.

Forgiveness

In the light of these circumstances, it can be very hard to come through to a place where forgiveness is possible. For many single parents, forgiveness is an issue that lies at the heart of their situation, before God, and in relationship with others, especially the other parent of their children. Some may need to know forgiveness themselves, for wrongs committed in the past, and to free them from the burden of guilt in the present. Others may need to forgive others for the hurts inflicted on them. For many, this process will take years, and it is vital that people do not expect forgiveness to happen quickly and painlessly.

Loneliness

Loneliness is a major issue throughout the whole of society. It is not confined to single parents, but can affect anyone. Our separation from both God and each other leaves us feeling isolated and vulnerable. The ultimate solution to this is the gift of God of the life, death and resurrection of Jesus.

Single parents can find themselves socially isolated, and unless people make a conscious effort to keep in contact with them, they can slip into the quiet despair of loneliness. Many single parents crave adult conversation, and this can be met by a Christian fellowship with a strong community network, especially by phone conversations, which can be a lifeline.

Expectations of relationships

Out of this need for intimacy and companionship can arise problems in looking for a potential partner. Single parents may easily believe that all they need is to find the 'right' partner and all will be set right, their needs for intimacy and companionship will be met and everything will be fine.

We all need to learn to find ourselves in Christ, and to seek strength, meaning and esteem from him. Sometimes, a single parent can only be ready for a new relationship when they are able to achieve fulfilment and happiness in their current circumstances.

4

Parenting Issues

24 hours a day, 365 days a year

Many churches are becoming more aware of the challenges and demands of parenting. This has resulted in a growing number of resources, courses and books on the subject. Single parent families face all the same issues as two parent families - together with other additional, unique issues.

Parenting is one of the highest human callings, and to be a parent is to carry out God's injunction to "be fruitful and multiply". Our culture often undermines the high priority that God places on being a parent, and tends to portray it as inferior to paid work.

The main difference between parenting with two people, and with one, is that someone on their own is parenting 24 hours a day.

Responsibility for the physical, emotional, financial, and spiritual well-being of children falls heavily on one pair of shoulders. There may be some assistance from the absent parent, but the parent with the day-to-day care has the lion's share. For many there will be no contact with the absent parent, and for others, erratic encounters that can be distressing. Some single parents have to cope with the extra demands of caring for children with special needs.

Finance

Lack of money is a serious problem for many single parents. Children are strongly influenced by peer pressure and if the parent is not able to give their children what others have, it can add to the parent's pain and feelings of failure. Everyday living can become a battle to keep within a tight budget. Holidays, birthdays, Christmas and leisure activities are all affected by this, and even church youth activities often involve subscriptions, uniforms, outings or camps. This lack of money can become the overriding issue for many single parents and can be the source of tremendous anxiety, on top of the sheer hard work of living with a limited income.

Superparenting

Parents want to give their children the best they can and to protect the children from as much pain as possible. This often results in the parent trying to be both mum and dad. This is an impossible task which adds to the pressures of single parenting and can undermine the self-esteem of a parent even more. While the needs of children are the responsibility of their mum or dad, parents should not have to meet all those needs directly themselves - others, such as schools, church and extended families can play their part, too.

The popular perception that vandals, muggers and other criminals all come from "broken homes" puts even more pressure on single parents. Many can feel that they are doomed to failure. Others try so hard to get it right with their children that they end up burnt out and exhausted. Often, single parents can feel that they are facing struggles in parenting because they are on their own, when in fact,

they are merely facing the common problems of being a
parent. It is important that they have contact with other
parents, including married ones, who can help them to feel
more 'normal'. What is really needed is acceptance, praise
and encouragement instead of criticism.

A balance of the sexes

Children can sometimes miss out on contact with one of the
sexes if they only have one active parent. If there are
opportunities for children to relate to other adults within
their extended family, or perhaps amongst friends and the
church, they will have role models to follow. Sometimes this
will involve a parent from another family taking a special
interest and developing a relationship with the child. For
example, a married man with children may be in a position
to 'extend' his fatherhood to cover the child of a single
mum. This does not mean that he will actually become this
child's father.   The traditional concept of a godparent
perhaps best describes this idea. Obviously there are
dangers to which children can be exposed by contact with
unsuitable adults who are given a place of trust. There is
also the potential that an inappropriate relationship could
develop with the single parent.   While bearing these
dangers in mind, it is important whenever possible for
children of single parents to have relationships with people
of the opposite sex to the parent they live with.

Fears and concerns

Parenting alone can be frightening, with fears for the safety
of the children heightened. Experiencing the loss of a
partner can create a need to cling tightly to what is left - the
children. Losing one parent means the child may fear losing
the other one too. It is possible to address some fears if there

is a strong, supportive community around: who is going to care for the child if the parent is ill or in hospital? Who can be phoned in the middle of the night if there is a crisis? Advice and guidance from other parents can be invaluable when asked for, and sharing with other parents can help when making decisions, and dealing with issues like the teenage years.

> "Many children are scared that the remaining parent will leave too. While playing in the garden, my 3½ year old screamed as though she had broken a limb. I rushed out to find that the back door had just blown closed and she was afraid I would leave her while it was closed."
>
> Jackie

Parenting takes time and energy and these may both be in short supply as the parent grapples with their own emotions, legal matters, job and practical responsibilities. If help is given in these areas, there will be more space for parenting.

Children's emotions

While the parent has much to contend with, the children also have their own difficulties. They have experienced loss too. The absence of a parent, whatever the cause, is a bereavement. There may have been other losses involved: home, family, friends, school, money, security, innocence. The child may go through feeling numbness, intense pain, sadness, anger, jealousy ("it's not fair"), depression, guilt, rejection or low self-worth. These may be very obvious or not surface for years and can cause quite extreme changes in behaviour.

Peter's losses (Aged 12)

- Mother - died.
- Father - physically (working long hours) and emotionally (coping with his own pain).
- Routine - frequent changes of carers, fending for himself more.
- Social activities - no one to take him to Scouts etc. Less opportunity to invite friends home.
- Balance and influence of women - very male household.

Some research suggests that children who go through their parents' separation are more prone to physical and mental health problems, educational difficulties and problems in their own relationships.[6] This of course does not mean that all the children of divorced or separated couples will encounter problems.

It seems that while some children withdraw into themselves or TV and computer game escapism (very common with teenagers), others become more demanding and are prone to emotional outbursts (especially younger children). The child may regress, or become defiant and manipulative. This can be difficult for any parent to cope with, but it is perhaps particularly difficult for those parenting alone.

'Baggage' from the past

What happened beforehand will also have a bearing. If the child's basic needs of security, self-worth and significance have been met, then he or she will be better equipped to cope with the present. If, for example, the child was abused and lived with violence in the home, this will obviously affect the single parent family, with the children perhaps being violent and abusive towards the parent they now live with, or other children. If they were taught to denigrate their mother, then they will not respect her or obey her now. If the disciplinarian parent leaves, then the other parent is faced with an unfamiliar role and possibly unruly children. Both the good and bad qualities and characteristics of the absent parent will live on in the children's lives.

Other children

Children easily feel "different". How much it matters that they are in a single parent family may depend on the local community. If they are in the minority, then teasing and bullying can occur. Jane was taunted with, "You are bad, ugly, horrid. Your daddy left you. He doesn't love you. You don't have a daddy." In fact, Jane's father had left her mother before she was born. Some children don't tell their friends about what has happened because they fear that they will not be treated as 'normal'. Betrayal, rejection or death can mean that the child finds it difficult to relate to and trust other children and adults.

Contact with the absent parent

Some children will have no contact with the absent parent. The child may feel that a part of them is missing. The finality of death can leave children desperate for any physical links, such as photographs or personal possessions. For those with no contact with living parents, there is a danger of substituting fantasy for reality. It is so important for all children to be given as much information as possible.

Contact with the not-at-home parent raises other issues. The child may be used as a pawn in an adult battle. He or she may have divided loyalties. There may be a swirl of emotions both before and after contact, with pleasure and excitement mixed with pain and disappointment. There may be expensive toys and outings, sometimes used by the absent parent in order to try to compensate for their lack of regular contact. The 'other' home may have different standards and rules. Often there is another partner. There may be half-siblings and step-siblings. Visiting has been described as stepping from the real, everyday world into an unreal one - a bit like being away on holiday in another country. Children may be forced to have contact when they don't want to, or be unable to have contact when they want to. They need to know that their needs are paramount.

Both parents are affected by contact times. The parent with everyday care may be terrified at what may happen to the children and there may be concern for the child's safety and welfare. They may feel lost without the children, or alternatively may welcome the opportunity for time and space for themselves.

The 'absent' parent cannot have the same relationship with the children as they had when they lived with them. This will be parenting at a distance and it can be upsetting to see your children being brought up differently to your wishes. Often it will be the father who is coping with the breakdown in his marriage/relationship and the loss of his children's daily presence. Sometimes the parent has nowhere to take the children, and contact centres where they can meet can provide a safe and inexpensive venue. Some churches provide this facility to families in their area.

Step-parents

Most children want their own blood parents to be the parents who care for them. If they cannot have them both, some children would rather have only one, and so it can sometimes be a particularly difficult time when a single parent starts a new relationship, or indeed marries. Often this will mean new brothers or sisters. This new relationship can of course be a source of great stability, love and nurture, but the relationship between a child or a teenager and a new step-parent can also be fraught with difficulties.

Positives aspects

Single parents sometimes tell us that there can of course be positive elements to single parenting too, even though this may not have been the way that they would have chosen.

Many single parents do a fantastic job, and speak of the fact that because of the adversity they face, they are drawn into a very close relationship with their children that lasts a lifetime. Money is often very short, and sometimes this means that the parent has to be innovative in building a relationship with their child.

Some single parents share that their marriage has been a bad experience. Becoming a single parent for them has meant freedom from violence or abuse, and a fresh start for the family.

It is often not until the teen years or early twenties that the child realises what sacrifices their parent has made and how deeply they have been loved, but we need to tell them now the value of the job they are doing.

In for the long haul

Parenting doesn't end when the children leave home. There may be weddings, and grand-parenting. Even if the single parent remarries, many of these issues will still be there - with the additional ones of step-parenting.

The emotional, physical and spiritual well-being of the single parent will have the greatest influence on the child's life. The support that we, the church, give will have a direct bearing on this.

5

Church Issues

Sunday morning....

Susan was determined that they were going to make it today. She got up early in order to give herself enough time, but after washing herself and the three children, with breakfast still to make, she knew it was going to be tight. Half an hour later, with everyone fed and dressed, James, her eldest son of seven, complained that he didn't want to go - he always got teased. While Susan was trying to calm his nerves, Katie spilled milk all over her dress, so she had to be changed. Susan and the children rushed out of the house to the bus stop 10 minutes before the service was due to start, knowing that the bus journey would take at least a quarter of an hour.

Their attempt to sneak in at the back of the service without being noticed was dashed by the baby, who let out a loud gurgle just as they were taking their seats, interrupting Mrs Jacobs who was leading prayers. As 30 people swivelled round to look at them, Susan could sense their disapproval.

When the children went off to the creche and Sunday School, Susan relaxed for probably the first time that week. The sermon was on parenting, which was very helpful, although the minister did go on about the importance of fathers. That was fair enough, but there was no mention of what to do when you are on your own. It left her feeling churned up inside. Why had he run off with that woman? She didn't understand. Was she just not a good enough wife, not good enough as a woman?

At the end of the service, the children were playing well with the others, so she had a chance to mingle over coffee. One of the elders came over and greeted her, saying, "We haven't seen you here in a while." Susan was crushed - he didn't seem to realise what an effort it was to get there. "When do you think you'll be coming to housegroup again?" Susan managed a smile and mumbled something about planning to come soon, but inside she was hurt: "How can I? Do you have any idea what that would take?"

"Do give me a call if you need any help!" he said. Susan was about to ask him if that included babysitting on Thursday night so that she could go to the housegroup, when she realised that he had been collared by the Youth Group leader - something about a summer festival.

Several of the mums were talking together at the back, and she was tempted to go over to have a chat, but the last time she joined that group she had felt such an outsider. It was as if they were unsure how to relate to her. She knew that many of them had found her divorce from Mike difficult to deal with - many of them had known them as a couple - but their ambivalence now was hard to take. "I need your friendship now more than ever - why are you pulling away from me like this?"

At the end of the morning, Susan felt deflated and insecure. Jane, who had two children and whose husband had died three years ago, was not there today, which was a pity, because Susan always felt safe talking to her. She was involved in leading the music group and had a good relationship with the church leaders, and she really understood Susan. Maybe she would give her a ring during the week. Jane had found herself more readily accepted and supported by the church, but was one of the few people who would give freely of her time when she could.

As the children came bounding back from Sunday School (they'd had a good time thankfully), she got them ready to go home, and as she packed them onto the bus, she wondered if coming to church was worth all the effort. She clicked back into 'mum' mode - what would they have for lunch, what did they need for school tomorrow, how could she cope with the budget this week...

Common experiences

Susan's experience may not be the experience of single parents at your church, but it is common enough.

There are notable exceptions; some churches are aware of and responding to the needs and opportunities which single parents present. However it has to be said that most single parents find they are not readily accepted in the local church.

The church has yet to grasp the magnitude of the issue of single parenting. In the average area covered by a local church, about 20% of all children under the age of 18 are now being brought up in a family headed by a single parent, usually the mother, and the numbers are increasing.

Social problems

Churches can sometimes assume that single parents have endless problems and don't have much to give to the local church. They may experience rejection in church because they are perceived as the following:

• Threatener: Their unmarried status seems like a threat to intact marriages.

• Failure: They are seen as having 'blown it' and incapable of managing their own lives.

• Alienator: They don't fit in with marrieds because they don't have spouses. They don't fit in with singles because they have children. They just don't fit in.

• Parasite: They are needy; "They will suck you dry." "They take, take, take and never give back." [7]

Most commonly, single parents are seen as a problem. Little thought is given to their potential as Christians and leaders. If any thought is given to their situation, it is usually only concerned with meeting the needs that they present, an approach that can easily wear out someone trying to help.

Typically in a church programme, single parenting, if it is considered at all, will be seen as a 'social problem' to be tackled in a separate slot of its own, instead of being integrated with the church's mainstream programme of teaching on relationships and parenting.

Why is this? The church has a long tradition of upholding marriage based family life and is absolutely right to prepare its members for this and to support them in it. The church also has some understanding of singleness, particularly when applied to young people and the elderly, and it is growing in its understanding of singleness as experienced by an increasing number of church members in between those ages. But it has difficulty in understanding those who are both single and parents and in working out where they fit into the local church. Many Christians waver between reactions of condemnation and pity, and struggle to forge genuine relationships.

With such high levels of marriage breakdown and births outside of marriage, it can seem as if family life based on marriage is under threat. The difficulty is that people can react to the single parents as if they themselves were the threat. In reality, the causes of family breakdown in the U.K. go much deeper than this, and only a minority of single parents made a conscious decision to become parents on their own.

Single parents often gravitate towards each other, forming fairly exclusive groups. While this can become very supportive if recognised and nurtured appropriately, it can also further isolate its members from the rest of the fellowship.

The need to value parenting within the church

It is vital that churches take the important task of parenting seriously and seek to support those who are parents in their fellowship and locality. Marriage, singleness and parenting all have integrity before God and this should be recognised in the local church.

There are several things that churches could do to help.

- People in the church could really seek to understand the life of the single parent.

- Single parents and their children could be identified and welcomed into the church.

- The needs of single parents in the congregation could be considered when planning teaching and ministry.

- Churches could consider how they might be able to meet some practical needs in the single parent's life.

- Opportunities for single parents to minister within the church should be created.

Ideally a church should have someone who understands single parents on its leadership team, so that the needs of, and opportunities for, single parents are included in the church programme. This could include specific activities to appeal to those who are outside the church. Time needs to be spent listening to single parents who can articulate how the church appears from their point of view. It is very difficult for someone who has not been in that situation to understand their life.

What is primarily required is the time needed to develop a relationship of trust, and the willingness to listen very carefully to what the single parent is saying about their life. It is also important for those who are parenting as part of a married couple not to impose solutions that work for them on to the problems faced by single parents.

Church life - single parent friendly?

Many church programmes are not 'user friendly' towards single parents. Parenting is often exclusively connected with marriage in a way that makes single parents feel alienated, and evening meetings are often very difficult for single parents to attend if they have young children, because of the cost of baby-sitting. Single parents, because of their background, may expect to be let down and may seem over-sensitive in their reactions to what they mistakenly take for rejection. It is vitally important then that attention is paid to removing any practical obstacles to involvement in the life of the fellowship. If there are mid week meetings, perhaps it would be possible to arrange babysitting rotas amongst parents, to enable people to attend. Would it be possible for someone living nearby to give the family a lift to church meetings?

The church can hold on to its traditions of teaching on marriage based family life as an ideal both within the church and in public life. But it also needs to develop teaching and ministry into situations which have arisen because parenting has become separated from marriage. Some of the consequences of this have been analysed in the section on personal issues. Many single parents have been through very painful experiences and need deep and sustained ministry from the church, as well as reliable long term friendships.

In the same way, it is important that a welcoming attitude is cultivated among members of the congregation, and this is likely to happen when it is effectively modelled by those in leadership.

It is difficult, but quite possible, with a little thought and a lot of encouragement, to integrate single parents into the life of a church and for them to grow into fruitful members of the Body of Christ. In the long run, the most valuable thing that a church could do would be to help single parents to an extent that they themselves were able to minister God's love and help both to other single parents and indeed to the rest of the church.

"I was left at the beginning of my pregnancy and discovered my husband's girlfriend was also expecting. At Christmas I was encouraged to send them presents of baby clothes, money and other sundries along with a letter professing my new found Christianity and my forgiveness for what they had done. Only recently I have realised that this may have resulted in over six years of no contact with his two children, and absolutely no help. I gave them every reason to believe that we were OK with what they had done. We must forgive, but it takes a LOT of time. How often church leaders in their eagerness to heal our hurts believe that praying about a situation deals with it for good and how upset they can become when we find it is not solved. Of course then we are made to feel guilty that there is something we are doing to prevent God giving us this instant healing. I thank God for all my friends that have listened to my harping on year in, year out, and been friends despite my depression. In being allowed to talk about it I am moving forward, and I know that I will eventually get over what's happened and move on. But it takes time. I feel angry now that at the beginning it was as if to be bitter and angry was almost a worse sin than that of an adulterous and abandoning husband. To be angry was 'to let the devil have a foothold.' 'Bitterness should never take root'. One elder, when I cried on the doorstep of the house I was being forced to move from, almost threatened me with, 'If you carry on with that attitude you will lose all your friends.' But my true friends did stick with me and allow me to feel normally and grieve."

Susan

6

Ideas for Churches

What kind of church do we need to have for children and single parents to feel welcomed, loved by God and other people, and supported through their emotional and practical difficulties?

Perhaps the best role for the church to take up in the lives of single parents is that of a partner - it can never be and should never try to be, spouse to a single parent, or a second parent to their children. The church is a partner who covenants with single parent families to enhance their family life, to strengthen their connection to systems outside of the family network, and to nurture and support their family faith journey.

It can provide commitment and friendship to single parents which, although not a substitute for marriage, can provide a different sort of love and companionship. This commitment can go a long way towards restoring the ability of a single parent to trust other people again. Sometimes another family in the church can extend itself to involve a single parent family. This inclusion is, of course, only partial but can be very helpful particularly if the children get on together. A further extension of the same principle might lead to a second tier of godparenting or sponsoring, where adults agree to be 'second godparents' to children of single parent families, with all the special interest and responsibility which that entails. The value of this exercise is that, while both families remain distinct, the single parent family can draw on the other family for advice and support. It has to be said that the number of families prepared to do this may be quite small, but it is an extremely effective way to help.

"Just this week a single mother came into the Way In. She had been walking the streets with her nine month old baby just so she could see people." Sheila, the co-ordinator of the 'Way In', a Peterborough project, tells of a recent visitor who found somewhere to go and someone to talk to.

The Way In began in a terraced house owned by the diocese, and rented at a reduced rate by two churches. The vision was to enable the members of Werrington Parish Church to reflect God's love in a practical way to the lonely and under-privileged in the parish. The theme of the project is neighbourliness.

The objectives include: providing an informal, home-like environment where people of all ages can meet, a listening and counselling service when requested, encouragement towards self-help, liaising with other agencies, providing a Christian perspective on family upbringing. On offer are drop in sessions for anyone, mother and toddler sessions, a thrift shop, and for the elderly lunches and teas.

"For single parents, we offer acceptance, friendship, a listening ear and a place to come to. Everyone is greeted with, 'Come on in and have a cup of tea.' It's meeting them where they are and with a non-

judgmental attitude. We can also call on the help of
other church members to help with debt counselling,
plumbing and carpentry. Single parents get together
and support each other," reports Sheila.

The following is a list - by no means exhaustive - of some of
the things that a church congregation can do to become a
more helpful place for single parents.

• Appoint an individual or some individuals on the church
  leadership team who are either single parents, or take a
  special interest in the lives of single parents. By
  cultivating relationships with single parents in the
  congregation, they will be able to learn what is going on
  in their lives and the lives of their children, and they can
  become trusted to consult with single parents about
  church decisions. These leaders can also be responsible
  for implementing some of the ideas that follow.

• Assign prayer partners to pray specifically for each single
  parent family on a regular basis. Make sure that these
  prayer partners are in regular touch with the family they
  are praying for so that they are aware of their prayer
  needs.

• Help financially. One single parent, who is a lay reader in
  her church, wrote to us about the social fund run by her
  church which can give grants and loans for advance rent
  and major repairs. It is available to anyone in the church
  who has attended for 6 months or more. Usually the
  person in need is referred by another church member. The
  decisions are made by any two members of a sub-
  committee.

• Have another look at the schedule of church meetings. Try
  to make these accessible to single parents - if you want

them to attend. Do they coincide with collecting from school, bedtimes, etc? If you have children, do you need a babysitter or your spouse to be with the children to attend these meetings? If so, they are inaccessible to single parents unless a babysitter is available. Why not create a babysitting service or rota within the church?

- Make sure that all the single parents you are in touch with have arrangements in place for emergencies. This is really important, and a very practical way to help. What happens if the parent is ill, or one of the children has to go to hospital? Who is there to look after the other children? A great burden of fear and anxiety could be lifted from the shoulders of many single parents if this is addressed. Find out whether the single parents in your congregation have any arrangements in place for emergencies. If there are any gaps - plug them!

- Stress the importance and integrity of marriage, singleness and parenting. Churches are used to parenting and marriage coming together in families, and it is important to stress how valuable parenting is, even if done only by one parent. Single parents can often feel isolated because they do not fit in to 'normal' family categories.

- Sometimes, it can be helpful to start a group for single parents to come together and share their experiences. This provides a valuable opportunity to meet with others who can relate and really understand, which will do much to combat the isolation felt by many single parents. If your church does this, it is essential that this is not all it does. When these groups are the only place where single parents are acknowledged and valued, there can be a tendency for them to become stereotyped and marginalised in the life of the church - a prospect most single parents would find quite frightening. Single parents need to be fully included in other aspects of the 'family' life of the local church.

• Children from single parent families can often feel isolated and, depending on the community they live in, face difficulties with their peer groups. Involve single parents' children in the youth work of the church. It may be necessary to seek them out and to keep on showing an interest, even when they don't really seem to respond.

• Make sure that your children's work is not run exclusively by either men or women. Some children really need contact with adults of the opposite sex to their parent. Within the work itself, it is important for the children's workers to be aware of the situation of the family, and to be careful with events such as Fathers'/Mothers' Day.

• Provide a practical resource to help single parents. Many people are extremely capable in home maintenance and car maintenance, for example, but others are not. A local church could provide a practical range of resources offered in an informal and non-patronising way and probably at no expense to the single parent. A pool of people with skills in carpentry, plumbing, electrics and car maintenance, who are prepared to help, would be an invaluable help to single parents and many others.

• Offer informal life skills courses on subject such as budgeting and DIY. Find out what skills people are lacking and whether there are people in the church who could provide basic instruction.

- Keep an eye out for the developing relationships between single parent families and other families in the church. If a special relationship with a safe, reliable church family is developing, the church could encourage this and pray for the two families on a regular basis.

- Use inclusive language. When teaching about marriage or parenting, be aware of the single parents in the congregation and the issues they are facing. If parenting is discussed, it would also be helpful to address the issue of parenting alone - use examples that single parents can identify with. Remember, single parents really need encouragement and praise, not criticism. They need to be affirmed, and the incredible job of raising kids alone should be recognised publicly.

- The following teaching subjects might be helpful:
  Emotions and how to handle them - anger, guilt, resentment, despair, rejection, loneliness.
  Forgiveness.
  Life skills: decision making, communication and conflict resolution skills.
  Parenting skills.

- Be very careful not to take on more than you are realistically able to do. With many of these situations, it will be better if you refer the person on to a suitable qualified Christian counsellor.

- Set up a specific ministry to single parents in your area. Many groups around the UK are starting to do this and are learning from their experiences. Some of the groups have set up a drop in centre for single parents and others, with a creche or nursery. Here, they have a chance to come in and meet with people to chat, get advice and information, and receive help with any specific problems they are experiencing. This can become an important part of the church's outreach and ministry to the community.

• Set up a resource for non-custodial parents to meet with their children, if they don't have direct access. A drop in centre or flat where parents and kids could go would be a useful resource for the community.

• Make sure that you do not assume that single parents are inevitably victims who need your help - recognise their leadership when it is there. In Bradford's Ripleyville estate, the single parents on the estate have been disproportionately more active than other groups in the regeneration of the estate. In fact, there have been times when the committee overseeing the regeneration work has consisted entirely of single parents.[8] One of the single mums involved now advises the government on housing policy.

• Take your commitment very seriously. Don't let it slip, or give up when things get tough. Many single parents are used to people letting them down, or not living up to promises made. By making promises that cannot be kept, you could be making the situation worse. Show radical commitment - don't give up.

• Tackle some of the root causes. Does your church offer support to marriages in your area? You could provide marriage preparation when people are getting married, support to all the married couples, even in the good times, and special help to couples who are going through hard times together.

Sarah is a 25 year old single parent with two children aged five and two years. About two years ago, Sarah became a committed Christian. The Pastor at her church tells us. "We recognised that she works very well with the church's young people - Sarah shows an empathy with their needs and the pressures of their peer group, yet also is able to stand up very clearly for Christ. We saw the possibility of using her talents and gifting on a broader canvas.

This summer she was thinking of trying to get a job, but really had no idea which direction to look in. The jobs she looked at were 'dead end' and she had no experience or qualifications to look more widely.

So our church applied to Fresh Start for Lone Parents at our local job centre, wondering if it would be possible to set Sarah onto a Training Scheme within the life of the church."

Training Scheme objectives were worked out and after negotiation, it was decided that Sarah could start work for one year. Her hours are 9.30am - 2.30pm with 2 evenings. She is allowed to keep her full benefits (including full rent payment for her house) and she also receives a full allowance for the cost of nursery school for her two year old which amounts to £60 per week. The church funds her expenses only.

7

Ideas for friends

We asked some single parents to make suggestions as to how their friends in church can offer really valuable help and support. Here are some of their suggestions, and a few of our own.

• Offer love, imagination and patience.

• Give your time.

• Ask what is needed, and suggest ways of helping. Don't just say, "Ring when you want something," - most people don't.

• Listen - don't be quick to give advice. Telephone calls with someone who is really listening can be a life-line.

• Provide some hospitality - meals, outings, cups of tea.

• Invite them on days out, holidays and family outings.

• Be there in the early days following death or separation. Help with the practical needs of living - cooking meals, washing and ironing, housework etc.

• Go to court, DSS offices, solicitors etc., to give some moral support.

• Be a friend - and listen. Often evenings (when the children are in bed), Sundays, Bank Holidays, Easter and

Christmas are the loneliest times. When the children are with the 'absent' parent, this again can be strange and lonely.

- Collect their child from school when the parent has dentist/doctor/hospital appointments.

- Be interested in the life of the children.

- Pray together about all concerns, especially the children.

- Help with the cost of extras like pocket money, school outings.

- Assist younger children to choose presents and cards for Mummy/Daddy for Christmas, Birthday, and Mothering Sunday - and pay for them.

- Look after parent and children when parent is ill - there may not be family close by.

- Invite them to go with you to church meetings and school functions. Sit with them in church.

- Offer lifts. Again, be specific - "Would you like a lift to.... on ....?"

- Don't criticise. Think why such and such might be happening; for example, if children are allowed to stay up late at night, this may be because their company is better than evenings alone.

- Encourage - let them know that they are doing a great and important job.

- Give them a chance to have a night off, by being available to babysit.

- Be discreet and imaginative with financial support.

- Giving some money well before Christmas could enable the parent to buy presents for the children.

- Notice things - there might not be another adult around to notice things like a new haircut or piece of clothing.

- Find out whether your friend has arrangements for emergencies. Could you be the emergency contact person in case anything goes wrong?

- Give gifts of small luxuries for the parent - chocolate biscuits or nice toiletries, the cost of a trip to the hairdressers.

- Value the single parent as a person in their own right who happens to be a single parent. Don't categorise them as a problem.

- Send cards and notes - they all say, "You are remembered".

- Recognise your friend's hopes and dreams and take them seriously. If they have any specific goals, see if there is anything you could do to help make it happen.

- Provide emotional support - recognise if your friend might need professional counselling. Pay for it if necessary.

- Remember important events and be interested - "How did the interview go?"

- Offer or help to arrange practical help with house maintenance - leaking taps, knocking in nails, gardening, especially the heavier jobs.

- Help in explaining 'the facts of life' to the children. A woman helping to explain periods to the daughter of a single parent dad could be very helpful!

- Remember this may be long term. Single parents still appreciate support and may have many needs even when they have been on their own for years.

- Be a committed friend. An uncommitted friend is worse than no friend at all - it just reinforces rejection, and the sense that you can't trust people. Keep your promises and hang in for the long haul. Commitment is what sorts the friends from the mere acquaintances.

8

Understanding your own Situation

It would be wonderful if there were a quick and easy set of solutions that could just be put into place within the life of the church that would make things easier, but the circumstances and talents of single parents are diverse - as are the size, gifts and abilities of different churches. It is important that you take the ideas in this book and use them not as a blueprint, but rather as a toolbox of ideas to draw from and apply in the most appropriate way. This section will help you to understand the situation of single parents in your church and area, and to consider the best way forward. For some of these questions, it may be helpful to write down your responses.

Single parents who attend your church
- Using the table overleaf, list the names of single parents who regularly attend your church. Note whether they live with their children, the number of children they have, how long they have been single parents and whether they are single parents because their partner has died, they are separated/divorced or they have never been married. Next to each of their names, estimate how much support they have from their own family. Put H for high, M for medium or L for low degrees of support. If you do not know any of these details, find out.

Name	Living with children?	Number of children	How long as single parent?	Why parenting alone?	Support from extended family?

- How well do you yourself know each of these people? What do you know of their situation, their needs, the issues they are facing? What are their gifts and talents? What issues do they face in their journey of faith?

- Do they have good relationships with other people in the church? Who are the people in your congregation who know them well?

- What is the church doing to help these people realise their potential as Christians? What practical obstacles do they face to becoming more involved?

- What do you think you can learn from them?

Other single parent families in the area
- Are you aware of other single parent families in the area where the church is ministering? What are their names, and where do they live?

- What are their needs?

Making church meetings 'user friendly'
- Do any of the single parents struggle to make it to meetings or groups that they would like to attend? Why is this, and what would be needed for them to be able to attend?

- If your church has home groups of any sort, are there any arrangements for babysitting rotas/sharing?

- Are single parents ever consulted about the organisation of church activities to check whether it would be accessible for them?

The wider congregation
- Have you had any feedback from single parents who have visited your church, or attend regularly? Were they made to feel welcome?

Teaching on marriage, parenting and family life
- If the church has a programme of teaching on family issues, does it include material which relates specifically to the situation of the single parent?

- Does it stress the enormous importance of parenting by single parents and married parents alike?

- Does the programme for single parents exist as part of an overall programme on the family or is it separated off in a way that might make single parents feel like a social problem?

- Do you run parenting courses or parent/toddler groups? How accessible are these to single parents?

Other resources
- There may be other organisations - either para-church, or local to the area - providing specific ministry to single parents, which single parents from the church could benefit from. Are you aware of these?

Family life
- Is the leadership aware of the practical problems which are a consequence of being a single parent family ?

- Can it provide a resource for the single parent who lacks a husband or wife in their own lives and fatherhood or motherhood in their families?

- Are there examples of extended families within the church?

- Are you aware of those single parents who do not live with their children? How might the church be able to help them develop those relationships and cope with the difficulties they face?

Ministry for single parents

- Are there members of the church who have been single parents or who have the experience of being brought up as members of single parent families? Would it be suitable for them to be encouraged to develop a ministry to single parents drawing, in part, from their own experience ?

- Would it be appropriate to start a group consisting mostly of single parents who would meet on a self-help basis? How would this be prevented from becoming a 'ghetto'? Who would be able to provide a positive lead to this group?

9

Suggested Resources

These suggested books, tapes and videos offer a variety of perspectives. Most, but not all, have a Christian basis. Inclusion in this reference list does not necessarily indicate endorsement by Care for the Family or by the authors of all the views expressed.

Please note that some books may go out of print or be temporarily unavailable. ISBN numbers are given wherever possible to assist in sourcing the items listed.

Single parenting

Sandra Aldrich, *From One Single Mother to Another* (Regal, 1991) 0 83071 480 4
A friendly, encouraging book which looks at loneliness, communication with your children, guilt, teenagers, and moving forward.

Jill Worth with Christine Tufnell, *Journey Through Single Parenting* (due to be republished soon)
A helpful book covering subjects such as loss, anger, loneliness, money, time, sexuality and remarriage.

Barbara Schiller, *Just Me and the Kids* (David C. Cook Ministries)
A complete resource kit for churches seeking to build a ministry to single parent families.

Lynda Hunter, *Single Moments* (Focus on the Family, 1997) 1 56179 532 1
Personal stories and thoughtful meditations to inspire and encourage single parents.

Sara Dulaney, *The Complete Idiot's Guide to Single Parenting* (Alpha Books) 0 02862 409 2
Advice on how to handle support, custody and childcare issues, daily schedules, financial and work issues, and remarriage.

Caryl Waller Krueger, *Single with Children* (Abingdon Press) 0 68739 555 5
Real-life stories with lots of useful tips.

Parenting

Celia Bowring, *The Special Years* (Hodder & Stoughton, 1997) 0 34068 672 3
A down-to-earth guide for parents with under five-year-olds.

Steve Chalke, *How to Succeed as a Parent* (Hodder & Stoughton, 1997) 0 34067 903 4
Ten top tips on encouragement, setting boundaries, learning to let go and much more.

Steve Chalke, *The Parentalk Guide to the Toddler Years* (Hodder & Stoughton, 1999) 0 34072 167 7
Easily accessible advice for the early years, including temper tantrums, sibling rivalry, and helping children make friends.

Steve Chalke, *The Parentalk Guide to the Childhood Years* (Hodder & Stoughton, 1999) 0 34072 168 5
Giving children self-worth; discipline; education; bullying, and much more.

Steve Chalke, *The Parentalk Guide to the Teenage Years* (Hodder & Stoughton, 1999) 0 34072 169 3
Learning which battles to fight; helping with career choices and boy/girl friends; and building self-confidence.

Paul Francis, *Teenagers: The Parent's One Hour Survival Guide* (Harper Collins, 1998) 0 55103 143 3
Shows how to help teenagers cope with today's pressures, with advice on possible problem areas.

Dr Ross Campbell, *How to Really Love Your Teenager* (Victor, 1977) 0 94651 522 0
Shows how to create a solid, balanced approach for relating to your teenager.

Gary Chapman and Dr Ross Campbell, *The Five Love Languages of Children* (Alpha) 1 89893 847 4
How to express love to your child in a way they can appreciate.

Karen Holford, *Please God Make My Mummy Nice!* (Autumn House, 1996) 1 87379 659 5
Humorous, honest reflections on real family life for mums under pressure.

Rob Parsons, *The Sixty Minute Father* (Hodder & Stoughton, 1995) 0 34063 040 X
Helping fathers to seize the day and find time for their children; to laugh more with their children; and to give love without strings.

Rob Parsons, T*he Sixty Minute Mother* (Hodder & Stoughton, 2000) 0 34063 061 2
Hope and encouragement for all mums, including loving and accepting your child; should I work or stay at home; single mothers; and why we often feel guilty.

Rob Parsons, *The Sixty Minute Parent* (Care for the Family, 1997)
Realistic advice and encouragement for all parents, on video. Including building strong relationships; the power of praise; and learning to let go.

Parentalk (Care for the Family, 1997)
Care for the Family's parenting principles course, containing a video, leader's guide and full colour course material for anyone wishing to run a parenting group.

Dr James Dobson, *The New Dare to Discipline* (Kingsway) 0 85476 803 3
The importance of consistent and fair discipline, with useful questions and answers.

Bereavement

Helen Alexander, *Experiences of Bereavement* (Lion, 1997) 0 74593 753 5
Insight into the grief process, and personal stories sharing a wide variety of experiences of bereavement.

Fiona Castle, *No Flowers ... Just Lots of Joy* (Kingsway, 1996)
0 85476 624 3
Fiona talks about her experiences when her husband Roy was diagnosed with cancer and subsequently died.

Fiona Castle, *Rainbows through the Rain* (Hodder & Stoughton, 1998) 0 340 1397 6
A collection of reflections, poems, prayers and songs to dip in to for encouragement during the hard times.

Janet Goodall, *Children and Grieving* (Scripture Union, 1995) 0 86201 866 8
For anyone helping children through the pain of bereavement, this book explains children's developing understanding of death, and how children go through the grieving process.

Jim Smoke, *Single Again* (Servant Publications, 1999)
1 56955 125 1

Divorce and remarriage

Andrew Cornes, *Questions about Divorce and Remarriage* (Monarch, 1998) 1 85424 396 9
The author describes his conclusion that remarriage should not be an option for those who are divorced, and also explores questions about forgiveness, reconciliation and singleness.

Mary Kirk, *Divorce - Living through the Agony* (Lion, 1998) 0 74593 804 3
Help for those experiencing the emotional suffering which follows separation and divorce, written by a marriage counsellor.

Piper, Curtis and Dobson, *How to Stay Sane when your Family's Cracking UP!* (Scripture Union, 1993) 0 86201 854 4
Helps young people to work through their emotions and cope when their family splits up.

Roger Smith & John Bradford, *Children and Divorce* (Church House, 1997) 0 71514 888 5
Looks at the legal processes involved in a divorce where children are concerned, and considers the needs of the children, the challenge to the church, how to help and who to turn to.

Jim Smoke, *Growing through Divorce* (Harvest House, 1995) 1 56507 322 3
Compassionate insights to help those facing the pain of divorce.

Steve Henshall, *Is This a Daddy Sunday?* (Monarch, 1994) 1 85424 253 9
A guide to help heal the scars of divorce which frequently affect extended family and friends, as well as the immediate family.

M. Scott Peck, *The Road Less Travelled* (Arrow, 1990) 0 099720740 4
Life lessons and personal spiritual growth.

Frank Retief, *Divorce* (Christian Focus Publications, 1998) 1 85792 421 5
Sexual frustration as a single; building a healthy marriage; reconcilation; what God says about divorce and remarriage.

Christopher Compston, *Breaking Up Without Cracking Up* (Harper Collins, 1998) 0 00274 001 X
'First aid' before, during and after the process of separation and divorce.

Finances and debt

Keith Tondeur, *What Christians Should Know About Escaping from Debt* (Sovereign, 1999) 1 85240 235 0
A booklet giving practical advice on debt.

Keith Tondeur, *A Family's Guide to Better Money Management* (Credit Action, 1995)
A small booklet offering sound, practical advice on family budgeting and handling money sensibly.

Step-families

Laura Walters, *There's a New Family in my House!* (Harold Shaw, 1995) 0 87788 810 8
Blending a new family together - exploring the confusing and powerful emotions and practicalities that can make life in step-families difficult.

Christina Hughes, *Step-parents, Step-children* (Kyle Cathie, 1995) 1 85626 082 8
Practical help for real issues - what if you don't love your step-children; discipline; coping with the 'ex'; what to consider when you want a child with your new partner.

Merrilyn Williams, *Stepfamilies* (Lion, 1995) 0 74593 383 1
Insights and advice to help build a stable, happy step-family.

T. Kahn, *Learning to Step Together* (National Stepfamily Association, 1996) 1 87330 917 1

Practical advice and solutions on issues such as strengthening the step-couple relationship, setting rules, building relationships with the children, and listening skills.

Tom and Adrienne Frydenger, *Stepfamily Problems: How to Solve Them* (Baker Book House) 0 80078 648 3

Forgiveness, rejection and loneliness

Johann Christoph Arnold, *The Lost Art of Forgiving* (Plough) 0 87486 950 1
A collection of stories showing the healing power of forgiveness.

Rev. Vera Sinton, *How Can I Forgive?* (Lion, 1991) 0 74592 010 1
Many people have problems with forgiving. This pocket book looks at forgiveness and the Christian faith.

Kevin Smith, *Explaining Forgiveness* (Sovereign World, 1996) 1 85240 125 7

Steve Hepden, *Explaining Rejection* (Sovereign World, 1996) 1 85240 077 3
Two booklets, each containing teaching and explanation.

Stuart Lees, *Will the Real Me Please Stand Up* (Hodder & Stoughton, 1997) 0 34068 675 8
Looks at personal growth and Christian discipleship, including real forgiveness and the healing of emotional hurts.

Prayer

Stormie Omartian, *The Power of a Praying Parent*, (Kingsway)
0 85476 640 5
How to pray through every age and stage of your child's life, with suggested prayers and Scripture verses.

Leanne Payne, *Listening Prayer* (Kingsway, 1994)
0 85476 558 1
How to hear from God.

Joyce Huggett, *Listening to God* (Hodder & Stoughton, 1996)
0 34064 170 3
Biblical meditation and using your imagination to enhance your prayer life.

10

Useful Organisations

Organisations marked * have a Christian basis.

*Association of Christian Counsellors
173a Wokingham Road
Reading
Berkshire
RG6 1LT
(0118) 9662207
www.doveuk.com/acc
email: office@acc-uk.org
Supplies details of Christian counsellors around the UK.

Big Brothers & Sisters
BCC House
2 Yukon Road
London
SW12 9UP
(020) 86754 2020
Provides carefully screened mentors for children from single parent families.

*Care for the Family
PO Box 488
Cardiff
CF15 7YY
(029) 2081 0800
www.care-for-the-family.org.uk
email: mail@cff.org.uk
Resources, events and family-building breaks to encourage parents and strengthen family life.

*CHEER
23 Calbourne Road
London
SW12 8LW
(020) 8673 1493
A local group which holds regular meetings for prayer ministry, teaching and practical support for single parents.

Child and Family Consultation Service
Dept of Child and Family Psychological Medicine
St Peter's Hospital
Guildford Road
Chertsey
Surrey
KT16 OPZ
(01932) 810298
Offers psychological help with problems which affect children.

*Child Link
Challenge House
29 Canal St
Glasgow
G4 0AD
0845 601 1134
email: cs@care.org.uk
A referral helpline on childcare issues.

*Christian Link Association of Single Parents (CLASP)
"Linden"
Shorter Avenue
Shenfield
Essex
CM15 8RE
(01277) 233848
email: office@clasp-charity.freeserve.co.uk
Support, encouragement, link penpals and a magazine for Christian single parents nationwide.

*Credit Action
6 Regent Terrace
Cambridge
CB2 1AA
(01223) 324034
Freephone helpline 0800 591084
www.creditaction.com
email: credit.action@dial.pipex.com
Free Christian financial advice, especially on getting out of debt.

Cruse Bereavement Care
126 Sheen Road
Richmond
Surrey
TW9 1UR
(020) 8332 7227
Support for anyone who has been bereaved.

*Divorce Care
57a Windsor Road
Forest Gate
London
E7 0QY
(020) 8534 7339
www.divorcecare.com
A Christian ministry to the separated and divorced, providing books, videos, tapes and courses.

*Family Caring Trust
8 Ashtree Enterprise Park
Newry
Co. Down
BT34 1BY
(01693) 64174
Parenting materials and courses.

*FLAME

(Family Life and Marriage Education)

Robert Runcie House

60 Marsham St

Maidstone

ME14 1EW

(01622) 755014

www.welcome.to/familylife

email: flame@csr.org.uk

Strengthening family life and marriage education.

*Fountain House

55 Spencer Park

London

SW18 2SX

(020) 8870 3707

Encourages families to host single parent families for Sunday lunch.

Gingerbread Association for Lone Parent Families

16-17 Clerkenwell Close

London

ECIR OAA

(020) 7336 8183

www.gingerbread.org.uk

email: general enquiry@gingerbread.org.uk

Support, social events and an advice line.

*Growing Through
3 Grange Road
Erdington
Birmingham
B24 ODG
(0121) 681 6855
Works with local churches to run workshops on single parenting.

*Listening Ear
44 Gayville Road
London
SW11 6JP
(020) 7223 5054
For single parents who just want to talk to someone.

*Marriage CARE
1 Blythe Mews
Blythe Rd
London
W14 0NW
(020) 7371 1341
A Catholic based organisation offering marriage preparation, marriage counselling, resources and a helpline.

*Mothers' Union
24 Tufton St
London
SW1P 3RB
(020) 7222 5533
www.themothersunion.org
email: mu@themothersunion.org
Offers 'Away From It All' (AFIA) holidays for families under stress who cannot afford a holiday.

National Association of Child Contact Centres
Minerva House
Spaniel Row
Nottingham
NG1 6EP
(0115) 948 4557
www.naccc.org.uk
email: naccc.org.uk
A nationwide network of contact centres which provide a neutral venue for contact when there is no viable alternative.

National Council for One Parent Families
255 Kentish Town Road
London
NW5 2LX
0800 0185026
email: info@oneparentfamilies.org.uk
A wide range of information and publications on benefits and tax, legal rights, holidays, maintenance, child support, returning to work, etc.

National Family and Parenting Institute
430 Highgate Studios
53-79 Highgate Rd
London
NW5 1TL
(020) 7424 3460
www.nfpi.org
email: info@nfpi.org
Provides a national focus on parenting and families, to support family life and help parents find the information and support they need.

Parentalk
PO Box 23142
London
SE1 0ZT
(020) 7450 9072
A range of resources and services designed to inspire parents to enjoy parenthood.

Parentline Plus
520 Highgate Studios
53-79 Highgate Rd
London
NW5 1TL
(020) 7209 2460
Freephone helpline 0808 8002222
www.parentlineplus.org.uk
A telephone helpline for parents and step-parents under stress.

*PCCA Christian Child Care
PO Box 133
Swanley
Kent
BR8 7UQ
(01322) 667207
www.pcca.co.uk
email: info@pcca.co.uk
Advice for those concerned about child abuse.

*Positive Parenting Publications
2a South St
Gosport
Hants
PO12 1ES
(023) 9252 8787
www.parenting.org.uk
email: info@parenting.org.uk
Leaflets and parenting courses on various aspects of parenting.

*Single Parent Network
c/o Care for the Family
PO Box 488
Cardiff
CF15 7YY
(029) 2081 0800
A network of various ministries across the UK, many of them specific to local areas, supporting single parents.

References

1. Social Trends 1998

2. General Household Survey 1995

3. *Divorce and Separation: The Outcomes for Children.* Joseph Rowntree Foundation, 1998

4. See the work of Markman and co. from the University of Denver, including *Fighting for your Marriage.*

5. *Divorce and Separation: The Outcomes for Children.* Joseph Rowntree Foundation, 1998

6. *Just Me and the Kids,* 1994, Singles Ministry Resources, David C. Cook Publishing, Colorado Springs, Colo

7. Yvonne Hutchinson, MCD Summer School Presentation, 1998